Tovoia

Imani Miner

Presentation by *BookLeaf Publishing*

Web: www.bookleafpub.com

E-mail: info@bookleafpub.com

ISBN: 9789357743662

First edition 2023

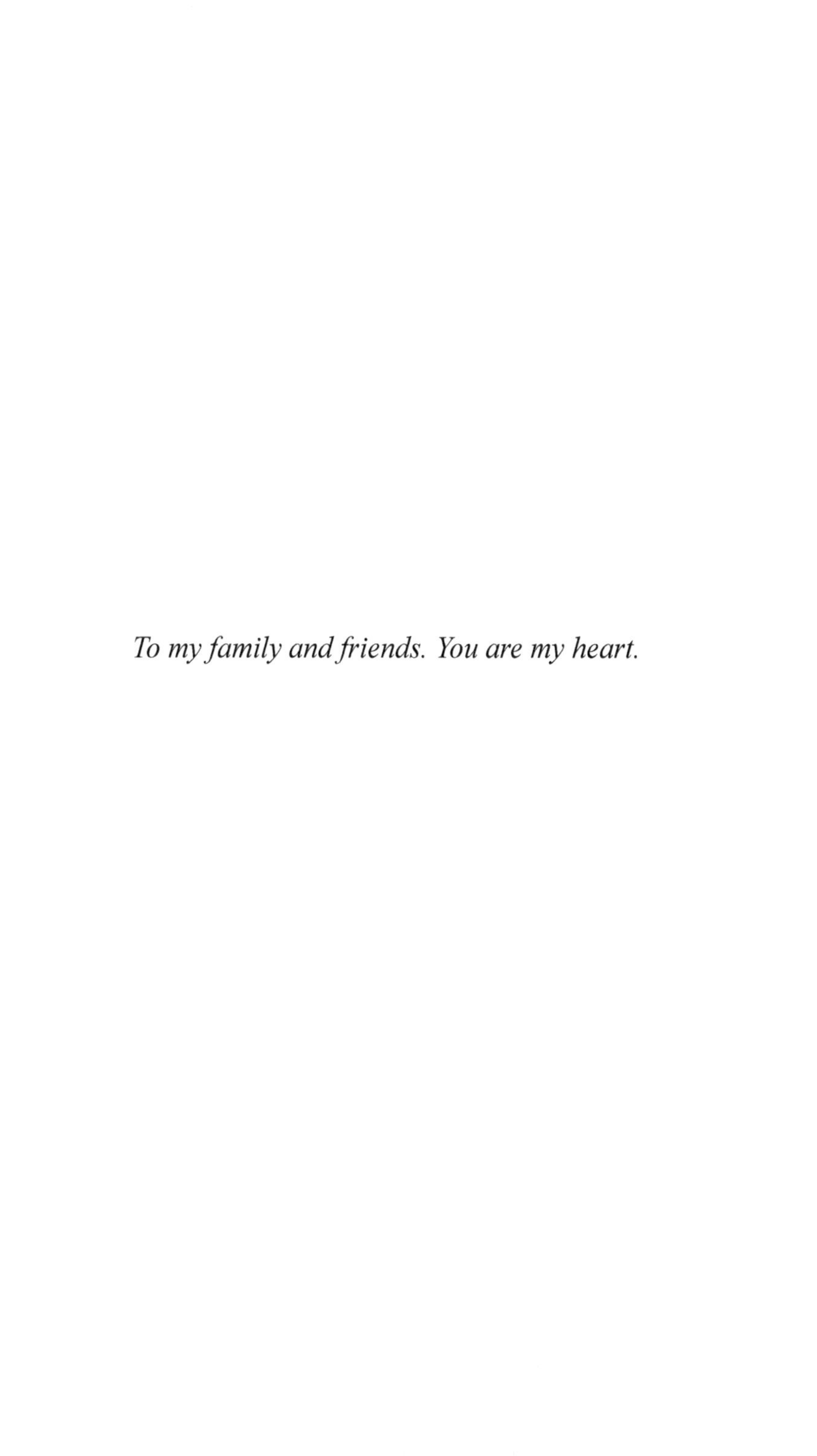

To my family and friends. You are my heart.

Sun Shone Upon Me

It was the kind of day
where the sun shone
upon the world
with blinding intensity
and shadows lay deep
and vast amongst
the unfathomable darkness.
The heat stroked the grass.
The flowers in the field.
The soft soil beneath my soles.
 The wind that cooled my skin.
More than enough for me.

Morning has no memory

The darkness of grief feels like a heavy blanket
draped over the streets of the soul.
Its chilly, damp presence creeps into the very
soul of my city.
It's blackness swallows up everything in its path,
leaving behind a void
of nothingness.
Memories remain.
They linger in the silence, refusing to be
forgotten but unable to be fully remembered.
Sleep is a comfort, until the rising sun brings
forth blinking and watery eyes to a new
morning.
1 year,
   5 years,
      17 years.
Morning has no memory
        of mourning.

To my mother

I will still love you midwinter.
Though the days are short.
When our skin is dry and lips chapped.
When time wears away; breaks our bodies.
When your thoughts give out.
I remember fall.
I recall spring.
The glow of life, blooming.
Your warmth.
I will remember the winter
and love you still.

Solace

I remember being young, younger than I can
recall,
stepping into a ritual older than time
sitting on couch pillows, some soft and some
worn with time,
stacked strategically on the living room floor
in between my mothers legs
while she performed a miracle on my soft, clean
and newly untangled hair.
the style would sometimes be complex and
sometimes simple.
In this place, there is a serenity I have never
known again.
I'd drift off to sleep, with my cheek resting on
one thigh, embracing the pain-to-numbness
feeling that had settled into my bottom, and I'd
dream of dragons, princesses, witches, and
heroes. I'd see angels, dive in the deepest seas
with no need to come up for air and meet a
mermaid or two.
I'd fly by sheer will to the highest of highs with
a satchel of stardust!

When I'd wake from these dreams of solace

a new ornate crown of woven hair and beads
would greet my smiling face.
I wonder, when she was in this place of peace
with her mother,
what she would dream of.

Mema brought the Sun

Mema brought the Sun in February.
A gift for me and you.
She asked the Sun to crack through the clouds.
The Sun answered.
It broke through the winter, and brought light
and warmth to the ground.
So that no matter where our feet land , we can
find refuge in her brightness.
Her gentle beams remind us
we're never alone.

Daddy's Rain

The rain has been a constant companion
since the day he left home.
Light drizzles dancing with
 the windshield
squeezed in the back seat
  no destination
  rhythmically pounding our little fists on the
roof for inflection
screaming
 I Wanna be Where You are OH!
Young lazy Sunday afternoons while Daddy
sings softly then loudly
*Keep your head to the sky *
Running under the blanket
giggling & whispering
creating an impenetrable fortress against the
thunderous night

Inner Child

8

Get in the way.
Get out.
The way of myself
is to destroy
my self-
worth until
i cannot hear
the child inside me
begging to eat.

11 years old

Air
 thick with anticipation
 the familiar scent of fried apples wafting to me
and Samaya's room.
Still caught in a dream,
 inexplicably elated and salivated
 swimming from the depths of sleep to the land
of the awake.
Fumbling from the top bunk, jogging to the
source of the aroma
 hear the bubbling
   the crackling
see fruits and syrup fusing together
the Sun haloing the face of a divine being
  spatula in one hand
  the other cradling
  a simmering pan
peek into its depths
and see the rhythm
   see me
   see us
   see life

Where

Where have you been?
I was searching for her in the woods
I searched indiscriminately
I searched boldly
heart racing
I shouted her name
through the hours
through the days
until my throat was strained and sore
with effort
I searched until I became clumsy
until my eyes blurred with tears
and then dried with time
until I could no longer see
I sat at the woodland edge
the journey heavy in my pockets
and sat in the stillness of twilight
the pounding in my heart now soft and gentle as
a stream
I peered into the heart of the stream
and there she was

The heart

thought this would be forever,
knowing it's not promised.
thought we were exempt.
an exception to the rule of heartache.
thought I paid my toll of agony early on.
the world doesn't stop to see if you're ok.
there's nothing to do but
break and bend.
crumble and mend.
again
and
again.

deep sleep

You own your mind
You walk with the voice of your heart
on your tongue
no apologies
Rooted in courage,
love
the wellspring of life overflows from you
Because of this,
you sleep
soundly
deeply
holy

honeysuckle

I will embrace this life.
I will step into this current of joy
pluck it like a honeysuckle in season
gently pinch and pull it's door
bring its nectar to my lips
suck the honey from my fingers.
I will not concern myself with
        inquisitive eyes or unwelcome visitors.
I will adore.
I will be adored.
I will seek.
I will be sought.
I will embrace this life.

Count the days

I've stopped counting the days
since the song of your soul
became a whisper
soft & faint
like a kiss
lingering on the skin
of remembrance

you and I

You and I own the sky
 all the wonders that she holds.
 We will never say goodbye
bathing in her pouring light of yellow-gold.
There are stars in you,
you know.
The kind that travel,
expand and grow.
I know that you can see
that there are stars in me.
You and I own the Sun
the Sun owns us too
When we embrace it's wonders
Can't tell if you are me or I am you.

Standing on the shore

the flickering lights of time
ever-changing
memories -turning in the river before you
rushing to the ocean
the ocean of words
calling you to re-join
the waves of grief
the guilt that holds you tight
when you stand on the shore.

This will take time

17

To Sorrow–
my porch is open.
pull up a chair.
here's a pillow for your back.
lean back and have a glass of iced tea.
Agave for taste.
Stay.
This will take time.

The man and the moon

I once knew a man
who grabbed the moon with his hand
as the stars screamed in protest
        so that I could know rest

For only one night
I woke up to the light
I knew he was gone
at the first sight of dawn

I once knew a man
who left with the moon in his hand
as the stars sang with glee
Welcome to eternity!

On Grief

Like 2 stones in my palm
bruised and cut from clasping
i'll have to go on
carry them like twins; rasping.

When the cuts get too deep
from their sharpness and mass,
I will stay awhile and weep
drop them & watch them shatter like glass

By the Road

Every year
  since childhood
  tulips bloom in my yard
 by the road; heavy with traffic
 (feet pounding the pavement
 cars whizzing by)
 when the light pours through the trees
  and highlights this brief and fleeting wonder
I am reminded of the gift of giving life
which never dies
but resurrects anew

Home

The house has been empty.
The walls can no longer hold us.
It cannot protect us from the wind.
       instead, it swallows us
       and buries us underground.

I will swallow the earth until
I rise to the welcoming sun
become a tree.
a home

Sister

22

I will be with you in moments of peace or joy.
I will sing your song.
I will bear witness to loss.
I will sit with you.
I will hold space in silence.
I will hold your hand.
I will honor your experience with compassion
as you did for me.